God's
lifting
Promises

by

David Marshall

First published 2004
Copyright © 2004
Reprinted 2005

All rights reserved. No part of this publication
may be reproduced in any form without prior
permission from the publisher.

British Library Cataloguing in Publication Data.
A catalogue record for this book is available
from the British Library.

ISBN 1-903921-24-4

Published by
Autumn House
Grantham, Lincs.
Printed in Thailand.

The Promises of God

*'No matter how many promises God has made, they are "Yes"
in Christ. And so through him the "Amen" is spoken by us to
the glory of God.'* (2 Corinthians 1:20, NIV.)

Jesus is the 'yes' to every promise of God.

* *We* say, 'It's impossible.'
  He says, 'All things are possible' (Luke 18:27)

* *We* say, 'I'm too tired.'
  He says, 'I will give you rest' (Matthew 11:28-30)

* *We* say, 'I can't go on.'
  He says, 'My grace is sufficient' (2 Corinthians 12:9)

* *We* say, 'I don't know what to do for the best.'
  He says, 'I will direct your steps' (Proverbs 3:5-6)

* *We* say, 'I can't cope.'
  He says, 'I will supply all your needs' (Philippians 4:19)

* *We* feel alone.
  He says, 'I will never leave you or forsake you' (Hebrews 13:5)

All texts are taken from the
New International Version unless indicated.
Other versions used
CEV = Contemporary English Version
KJV = King James Version
MGE = The Message
NASB = New American Standard Bible
NLT = New Living Translation
REB = Revised English Bible

In the natural world confidence is self-reliance.
In the spiritual world it is God-reliance.

'Keep on being brave!
It will bring you great rewards.'

Hebrews 10:35, Contemporary English Version.

God has armed you so that you will go through suffering, not without pain, but without stain. But he wants you well.

'The prayer offered in faith will make the sick person well.'

James 5:15.

Those who go to live in heaven when Jesus comes will have heaven within them now.

'In just a very little while,
"He who is coming will come
and will not delay." '

Hebrews 10:37.

Because joy is the serious business of heaven, it is our business as we prepare for heaven.

'All who keep the Sabbath without desecrating it and who hold fast to my covenant – these I will bring to my holy mountain and give them joy in my house of prayer.'

Isaiah 56:6, 7.

Embrace your freedom!

---

*'Christ has set us free to live
a free life. So take your stand!
Never again let anyone put
a harness of slavery on you.'*

Galatians 5:1, MGE.

Sin-sorrow leads to the bridge called Forgiveness; and beyond that bridge is heaven.

'If we admit our sins – make a clean breast of them – he won't let us down; he'll be true to himself. He'll forgive our sins and purge us of all wrongdoing.'

1 John 1:9, MGE.

God is your Pace-setter, so don't rush.
God is your Time-keeper, so be still, be calm.
And God is ever present to bring you peace.

———————————

*' "I will be with you; I will not
fail you or forsake you." '*

Joshua 1:5, NASB.

Your back up against it? There is a way of escape.
No place to hide? God is your refuge.

'The Lord will be a refuge for his people.'

Joel 3:16.

Don't sweat. Don't wrestle.
It's not a case of TRY, but TRUST.

'For he loves us with unfailing love;
the faithfulness of the Lord
endures for ever.
Praise the Lord!'

Psalm 117:2, NLT.

It's impossible? Christians are put into the world to do the impossible – in the strength of God.

' "Everything is possible for him who believes." '

Mark 9:23.

Have you been wronged?
Do you have a sense of injustice?
God understands.
One day all wrongs will be righted.

God 'will judge your people in righteousness, your afflicted ones with justice'.

Psalm 72:2.

God wants the very best for the uttermost, the outermost, the whosoever will.

' "Whoever is thirsty, let him come; . . . let him take the free gift of the water of life." '

Revelation 22:17.

Ground between the millstones of temptation?

'Since he himself has gone through suffering and temptation, he is able to help us when we are being tempted.'

Hebrews 2:18, NLT.

Intimidated by the future?
The only light upon the future is faith.

---

*'For the Lord will go before you,
and the God of Israel will be
your rearguard.'*

Isaiah 52:12, NASB.

Isolated, deserted, left behind?
Help is on the way.

_____

'Behold, the Lord God
will come with might,
With His arm ruling for Him.
Behold, His reward is with Him
And His recompense before Him.'

Isaiah 40:10, NASB.

Strive, seek, find – and don't give up!

'Some so-called prayer warriors ...
are prayer ignorant. They're full
of formulas and programmes and
advice, peddling techniques for
getting what you want from God.
... This is your Father you are
dealing with, and he knows better
than you what you need.'

Matthew 6:7-9, MGE.

Blessed are the pushy,
the assertive, the bullies? No way!
The Jesus Agenda favours those who
realise their utter helplessness.

---

*'The meek will inherit the land
and enjoy great peace.'*

Psalm 37:11.

*'Blessed are the meek,
for they will inherit the earth.'*

Matthew 5:5.

Are you nearing the edge?
Don't look down!
Look up!

' "You're blessed when you're at the end of your rope. With less of you there is more of God and his rule." '

Matthew 5:3, MGE.

' "My power works best in your weakness." '

2 Corinthians 12:9, NLT.

God doesn't send trials,
though he may permit them – if you're in good shape.
God doesn't send temptation.
But he's the source of your succour in temptation.

_____

'Don't let anyone under pressure
to give in to evil say,
"God is trying to trip me up."
God is impervious to evil,
and puts evil in no one's way.'

James 1:13, MGE.

Christ is the best inheritance.

---

*'If you belong to Christ, then you are
... heirs according to the promise.'*

Galatians 3:29.

*'In his great mercy he has given
us new birth into a living hope ...
and into an inheritance that can
never perish, spoil or fade
– kept in heaven for you.'*

1 Peter 1:3, 4.

Present tense? Future certain.
The fairest sights? The sweetest strains?
The deepest joys?
You ain't seen nothing yet.

———————————

' "No eye has seen, no ear has heard, no mind has conceived what God has prepared for those who love him." '

1 Corinthians 2:9.

Is your life arid, your surroundings sterile?
Become a seeker!

---

*'Those who seek the Lord
lack no good thing.'*
Psalm 34:10.

*'I [God] will send down showers
in season; they will be
showers of blessing.'*
Ezekiel 34:26.

On your lonesome and up against it?
Open the door to your Visitor. . . .

_____

Jesus said, ' "Be sure of this:
I am with you always,
even to the end of the age." '

Matthew 28:20, NLT.

Pulled in all directions?
Too many voices?
Doubt self and trust God.

'In all your ways acknowledge him,
and he will make your
paths straight.'

Proverbs 3:6.

Total trust is the route to total contentment. And total trust only comes to those who live life in the will of God.

'God will meet all your needs according to his glorious riches in Christ Jesus.'

Philippians 4:19.

To have more, desire less.
Beware lest you lose the substance
by grasping at shadows.

---

*'A righteous man may
have many troubles,
but the Lord delivers him
from them all.'*

Psalm 34:19.

There is only one person God cannot forgive.
The person who refuses to come to him
for forgiveness.

' "I [God] will forgive
their wickedness and will
remember their sins no more." '

Hebrews 8:12.

Forgiveness does not mean that God cancels
the consequences of wrongdoing.
It means that God has refused to allow our
guilty past to affect his relationship with us.

'He has removed our rebellious acts as far away from us as the east is from the west.'

Psalm 103:12, NLT.

God whispers in our pleasures,
shouts in our pain – but, in both,
in reassuring tones, he says,
'Better times are coming.'

'I heard a voice thunder from the Throne: "Look! Look! God has moved into the neighbourhood, making his home with men and women! They're his people, he's their God. He'll wipe every tear from their eyes. Death is gone for good – all the first order of things gone . . . . Look! I'm making everything new." '

Revelation 21:3-5, MGE.

Being smothered and suffocated by a sense of guilt?

_____

' "This is the brand-new covenant.
. . . I will put my law within them
– write it on their hearts!
– and be their God.
And they will be my people. . . .
They'll know me firsthand,
. . . the smart and the slow.
I'll wipe the slate clean
for each of them.
I'll forget they ever sinned!"
God's Decree.'

Jeremiah 31:33, 34, MGE.

Though God can forgive and forget your sins,
he cannot forget you.

_____

*'I will not forget you!
See, I have engraved you
on the palms of my hands.'*

Isaiah 49:15, 16.

In a teeming, shifting, uncertain world there is one thing you can depend on.

'God is our God for ever and ever; he will be our guide even to the end.'

Psalm 48:14.

Ｇod will spare the sinner because he
did not spare his Son.

'Become friends with God;
he's already a friend with you.
How? you say. In Christ.
God put the wrong on him who
never did anything wrong,
so we could be put right with God.'

2 Corinthians 5:20, 21, MGE.

Get your priorities right –
and get things in perspective!

'People who don't know God and
the way he works fuss, . . . but you
know both God and how he works.
Steep your life in God-reality,
God-initiative, God-provisions.
Don't worry about missing out.
You will find all your everyday
human concerns will be met.'

Matthew 6:31-33, MGE.

The Christian who is lonely is in the ridiculous position of being backed by the whole of Christendom, and Christendom's God.

'The angel of the Lord encamps around those who fear him, and he delivers them.'

Psalm 34:7.

Overwhelmed by trouble?
It has 'come to pass', not to stay.
In the east, the dawn is breaking....

---

*'Weeping may remain for a night,
but rejoicing comes
in the morning.'*

Psalm 30:5.

When we think of the mountains, the rivers and the cities – the world seems empty. Peer through a telescope across the seemingly limitless expanses of space – and the universe seems empty.
Yet we know someone who thinks and feels with us, is close to us in spirit, and has offered to shoulder any of the problems that we find just too much.

' "Is anything too hard for the Lord?" '

Genesis 18:14.

There is a native, homing instinct in our souls which turns us to God as naturally as the flower turns to the sun. And, when we have turned to God, he gives us faith – the only means of certainty in an uncertain world.

_____

' *"Everything is possible for him who believes."* '

Mark 9:23.

' *"If? There are no 'ifs' among believers. Anything can happen."* '

Mark 9:23, MGE.

Trust the past to God's mercy,
trust the present to God's love,
trust the future to God's providence.

---

*'Trust in the Lord and do good;
settle in the land and
find safe pasture.
Delight in the Lord,
and he will grant you
your heart's desire.'*

Psalm 37: 3, 4, REB.

What soap is to the body, tears are to the soul.
When you reach the place of tears
you know that your spirit has escaped
from the imprisonment of this world –
and set its foot upon the path to the next.

_____

*'Those who sow in tears will
reap with songs of joy.'*

Psalm 126:5.

A smooth sea has never made a skilful mariner,
neither do uninterrupted prosperity and success
qualify for usefulness and happiness.
The storms of adversity rouse the faculties,
excite the invention,
skill and fortitude of the voyager.

'The Lord is close to the
broken-hearted and saves
those who are crushed in spirit.'

Psalm 34:18.

The great thing about fearing God is that when you fear God you fear nothing else.

'Start with God – the first step in learning is bowing down to God; only fools thumb their noses at such wisdom and learning.'

Proverbs 1:7, MGE.

'Fear of the Lord is the beginning of knowledge. Only fools despise wisdom and discipline.'

Proverbs 1:7, NLT.

We sleep peacefully in God's arms when we yield ourselves to God's providence.

'The Lord will go before you, your rearguard will be Israel's God.'

Isaiah 52:12, REB.

You are not tempted because you are evil;
you are tempted because you are human.

_____

'Thanks be to God!
He gives us the victory
through our Lord Jesus Christ.'

1 Corinthians 15:57.

1 TREE + **3** NAILS = **4** GIVEN

'Jesus said, "Father, forgive them,
for they do not know what
they are doing." '

Luke 23:34.

God casts confessed sins into
the deepest part of the ocean –
and leaves a 'no fishing' sign over the spot.

---

*'Praise the Lord, . . . who forgives
all your sins and heals
all your diseases.'*

Psalm 103:2, 3.

We may feel alone and isolated but the central message of Scripture is this: God cares! God will never abandon you!

'The Lord watches over the alien and sustains the fatherless and the widow.'

Psalm 146:9.

Hope is hearing the music of the future;
and faith is moving to its rhythm.

' "This same Jesus,
who has been taken from you,
. . . will come back." '

Acts 1:11.

Friendships begun here will be taken up again elsewhere, never to be broken off.

'Whoever turns a sinner from the error of his way will save him from death.'

James 5:20.

Hope is not the belief that something
is going to turn out right;
it is the certainty that something makes sense,
regardless of how it turns out.

———————————————

'Those who wait on the Lord
will find new strength.
They will fly high on wings like eagles.
They will run and not grow weary.
They will walk and not faint.'

Isaiah 40:31, NLT.

Griefs exalt us, troubles lift us –
and all our troubles are sifted
through the fingers of Christ.

---

*'I will say of the Lord, He is
my refuge and my fortress:
my God; in him will I trust.'*

Psalm 91:2 KJV.

God is prepared to wait for your decision.

'God isn't late with his promise as some measure lateness. He is restraining himself on account of you, holding back the End because he doesn't want anyone lost.'

2 Peter 3:9, MGE.

The only thing you need in order to pray
is a sense of your openness to God.
The self-sufficient do not pray,
the self-satisfied will not pray,
and the self-righteous cannot pray.

_____

'When you pray, go away by
yourself, shut the door behind you,
and pray to your Father secretly.
Then your Father, who knows all
secrets, will reward you.'

Matthew 6:6, NLT.

The best things in life *are* free!

'God loves us so passionately
he gave us some slack and let
the Liberator [Jesus] resuscitate
our spiritual side that had
been throttled by our mess.
Free, no charge, a gift –
God's OTT generosity is what's
straightened you out.'

Ephesians 2:7, 8, STREET BIBLE.

What God has done once, he can do again:
come to this planet in Person.

---

*'Grace and peace be to you
from him who is and who was
and who is coming.'*

Revelation 1:4, Phillips.

Heaven is not far away.
It's within speaking distance
twenty-four hours a day, seven days a week.

'Before they call, I will answer;
and while they are yet speaking,
I will hear.'

Isaiah 65:24, KJV.

The great tragedy of life is not unanswered prayer; it is unoffered prayer. So pray, why don't you?

'I pleaded with the Lord . . .
But he said to me,
"My grace is sufficient for you,
for my power is made perfect
in weakness." '

2 Corinthians 12:8, 9.

Need company for a spiritual retreat?

' "Are you tired? Worn out? Burned out on religion? Come to me. Get away with me and you'll recover your life. I'll show you how to take a real rest. . . . watch how I do it. Learn the unforced rhythms of grace. . . . Keep company with me and you'll learn to live freely and lightly." '

Matthew 11:28-30, MGE.

Are you facing the impossible?
That's God's territory!

---

*'Nothing is impossible
with God.'*

Luke 1:37.

Don't just sit there: pray something!
Coincidences happen when you pray.

'A good man's prayer is very powerful and effective.'

James 5:16, REB.

God is no man's debtor.

'He who walks righteously . . .
his bread will be supplied,
and water will not fail him.'

Isaiah 33:15, 16.

No burden is too great for God to take from your shoulders.

'Praise be to the Lord,
to God our Saviour,
who daily bears our burdens.'

Psalm 68:19.

The Word, you can depend on:
lay hold on it until it lays hold on you.

_____

' "Heaven and earth will pass away,
but my words will never
pass away." '

Matthew 24:35.

Humility is being able to laugh at yourself.
And God rewards the humble.

---

*'The Lord takes delight in
his people; he crowns the
humble with salvation.'*

Psalm 149:4.

God empowers you
when you make a clean break.

'Quit dabbling in sin.
Purify your inner life.
Quit playing the field.'

James 4:8, MGE.

The only way to walk tall is to get on your knees first.

'Hit bottom, and cry your eyes out.
The fun and games are over.
Get serious, really serious.
Get down on your knees before
the Master; it's the only way you'll
get on your feet.'

James 4:9, 10, MGE.

God does down the proud and rewards the humble.

' "God goes against the wilful proud; God gives grace to the willing humble." So let God work his will in you. Yell aloud no to the Devil and watch him scamper. Say a quiet yes to God and he'll be there in no time.'

James 4:6, 7, MGE.

B e healthy – and holy! – by God's creation!

'May God himself, the God who makes everything holy and whole, make you holy and whole, put you together – spirit, soul, and body – and keep you fit for the coming of our Master, Jesus Christ. The One who called you is completely dependable. If he said it, he'll do it!'

1 Thessalonians 5:23, 24, MGE.

God comforts you: it's his role.
You comfort others: it's your role.

'God ... comforts us in all our
troubles, so that we can
comfort those in any trouble.'

2 Corinthians 1:3, 4.

If you have your hand in the hand of God . . .

'Stalwart walks in step with God;
his path blazed by God, he's happy.
If he stumbles, he's not down for long;
God has a grip on his hand.'

Psalm 37:23, 24, MGE.

Every tomorrow has two handles. We choose which one we use. We can take hold of tomorrow by the handle of anxiety, or by the handle of faith.

'The Lord is near; do not be anxious, but in everything make your requests known to God in prayer . . . . Then the peace of God, which is beyond all understanding, will guard your hearts and your thoughts in Christ Jesus.'

Philippians 4:5-7, REB.

There are no limits to God's power.

'For I am convinced that neither death nor life, neither angels nor demons, neither the present nor the future, nor any powers, neither height nor depth, nor anything else in all creation, will be able to separate us from the love of God that is in Christ Jesus our Lord.'

Romans 8:38, 39.

God has a 100% success rate.

'Praise be to the Lord, . . . Not one word has failed of all the good promises he gave.'

1 Kings 8:56.

Happiness depends on what happens; joy does not. Joy follows freedom.

'The Lord's people, set free, will come back . . . with everlasting joy. Gladness and joy will come upon them, while suffering and weariness flee away.'

Isaiah 35:10, REB.

Only the armour of God makes the soul impregnable.

'Find your strength in the Lord, in his mighty power. Put on the full armour provided by God, so that you may be able to stand firm against the stratagems of the devil.'

Ephesians 6:10, 11, REB.

Suffering makes us either bitter or better; it is inevitable. Only misery is optional.

———————————————

' "My child, don't ignore it when the Lord disciplines you, and don't be discouraged when he corrects you. For the Lord disciplines those he loves.'

Hebrews 12:5, 6, NLT.

Nobody cares what becomes of you? *God cares.*
And with an infinite tenderness.
He cared before you cast your care on him.

God 'cares for you, so cast all your anxiety on him'.

1 Peter 5:6, REB.

If you spend your whole life waiting for the storm, you'll never enjoy the sunshine.

'Humble yourselves . . . under God's mighty hand, and in due time he will lift you up.'

1 Peter 5:6, REB.

Anxiety is the rust of life, destroying its brightness and weakening its power. The antidote to anxiety is trust.

' "Set your troubled hearts at rest. Trust in God always; trust also in me. There are many dwelling-places in my Father's house. . . . I shall come again and take you to myself, so that where I am you may be also." '

John 14:1-3, REB.

Worry is interest paid on trouble
before it falls due.

' "Peace is my parting gift to you,
my own peace,
such as the world cannot give.
Set your troubled hearts at rest,
and banish your fears." '

John 14:27, REB.

He who is not contented with what he has would not be contented with what he would like to have.

' "I have told you all this so that
in me you may find peace.
In the world you will have suffering.
But take heart!
I have conquered the world." '

John 16:33, REB.

The one who provides for this life
but not for eternity
is wise for an instant, but a fool for ever.

---

*'Keep yourselves in the love of
God, and look forward to the day
when our Lord Jesus Christ in his
mercy will give eternal life.'*

Jude 21, REB.

Only one thing lasts for eternity.
Feelings pass. Opinions change.
The work done for Christ lasts for ever.

———————————

*' "You are my witnesses,"
declares the Lord,
"and my servant
whom I have chosen." '*

Isaiah 43:10.

Pray – then wait.
The highest attainment in life is to remain still
long enough to allow God to speak to you.

'If you stray from the path,
whether to right or to left, you will
hear a voice from behind you
sounding in your ears saying,
"This is the way; follow it." '

Isaiah 30:21, REB.

Do what you can, with what you have,
where you are.

'If you do not stand firm in your
faith, you will not stand at all.'

Isaiah 7:9.

Eternity is the place where questions
and answers become one.

---

*'What I do thou knowest not now;
but thou shalt know hereafter.'*

John 13:7, KJV.

God is ultimate security.

'*God is bedrock under my feet,*
the castle in which I live,
my rescuing knight.
My God – the high crag
where I run for dear life,
hiding behind the boulders,
safe in the granite hideout.'
Psalm 18:1, 2, MGE.

Don't pray to be sheltered from dangers;
but to be fearless in facing them.

' "When you pass through the
waters, I will be with you;
and when you pass through the
rivers, they will not sweep over you.
When you walk through the fire,
you will not be burned; . . .
For I am the Lord, your God." '

Isaiah 43:2, 3.

It is better to walk with God in the dark
than to walk alone in the light.

---

*'Let him who walks in the dark,
who has no light, trust in the name
of the Lord and rely on his God.'*

Isaiah 50:10.

In trouble or despair?
Do what David did: pour out your heart to God.

_____

*'If you call to me in time of trouble,
I shall come to your rescue.'*

Psalm 50:15, REB.

When you are intimidated by death . . .

_____

'Jesus says, "I'm the Death of Death. I'm Life with a capital 'L'. Invest all you've got in me and you'll live, and that includes dead people. You put it all on the line for me and you'll never die." '

John 11:25, 26, STREET BIBLE.

Hang in there!

'Happy is the man who stands up to trial! Having passed that test he will receive in reward the life which God has promised to those who love him.'

James 1:12, REB.

Is it all getting too much for you?

_____

'Pile your troubles on God's shouders
– he'll carry your load.'

Psalm 55:22, MGE.

Sorrow is lent, not given.
Because it is lent, it may be taken away.

' "Your days of sorrow will end." '

Isaiah 60:20.

If it's a case of not *what* you know but *who* you know, then make sure you know the right Person!

_____

'I know the one in whom I trust, and I am sure that he is able to guard what I have entrusted to him until the day of his return.'

2 Timothy 1:12, NLT.

Worried about what's happening?
Don't! God will work it out.

'In all things God works for the good of those who love him.'

Romans 8:28.

We are all called to take part in a struggle.
And in that struggle, prayer is the supreme weapon.

'Submit yourselves, then, to God.
Resist the devil,
and he will flee from you.'

James 4:7.

The prospect is not as distant as you may think.

' "Never again will they hunger; never again will they thirst. . . . God will wipe away every tear from their eyes." '

Revelation 7:16, 17.

The only way to learn strong faith
is to endure great trials.

---

*'The Lord knows how to rescue
godly men from trials.'*

2 Peter 2:9.

Choked by pessimism?

' "Behold, I will create new heavens and a new earth." '

Isaiah 65:17.

Those who stick at it will be rewarded.

'You were sure of yourselves then. It's still a sure thing! But you need to stick it out, staying with God's plans so you'll be there for the promised completion.'

Hebrews 10:36, MGE.

God sticks by his friends.

---

*'The Lord is good
to those whose hope is in him,
to the one who seeks him.'*

Lamentations 3:25.

God's love is a love without angles:
a love that redeems.

'Give thanks to the Lord,
for he is good;
his love endures for ever.'

Psalm 107:1.

The world is a ship, not an iceberg.
There is someone at the controls;
it is not a runaway.

'In just a very little while, "He who is coming will come and will not delay. But my righteous one will live by faith." '

Hebrews 10:37.

There are anxious times for us all.
There are times of weakness.
But in those times God carries us.

———————————

'Give all your worries to God, . . .
he cares about what
happens to you.'

1 Peter 5:7, NTL

Walk in God's way, depend on God's blessing
– and find yourself empowered.

---

*'The Lord your God will bless you
in all your work and in everything
you put your hand to.'*

Deuteronomy 15:10.

On call: a source of
help and encouragement 24/7.

---

*'I call to God;
God will help me.
At dusk, dawn, and noon I sigh
deep sighs – he hears,
he rescues.'*

Psalm 55:16, MGE.

God has everything in hand.

---

*'God holds the high centre,
he sees and sets the world's mess
right. He decides what is right for
us earthlings, gives people their
just deserts.'*

Psalm 9:7, 8, MGE.

God makes things make sense.

'*Keep me safe, O God,*
I've run for dear life to you.
I say to God, "Be my Lord!"
Without you,
nothing makes sense.'

Psalm 16:1, 2, MGE.

God will be your hiding place
when there is no other.

---

*'He who dwells in the shelter of
the Most High will rest in the
shadow of the Almighty.'*

Psalm 91:1.

At the centre of the universe
a heart of love beats.

---

*'A hostile world! I call to God,
I cry to God to help me.
From his palace he hears my call;
my cry brings me right into his
presence – a private audience!'*

Psalm 18:6, MGE.

God is dependable in all circumstances.

---

*'He pulled me out
of that ocean of hate,
that enemy chaos, the void
in which I was drowning.
They hit me when I was down,
but God stuck by me.'*

Psalm 18:16, 17, MGE.

Aim right – and you can't miss!

---

*'What a God! His road
stretches straight and smooth.
Every God-direction is road-tested.
Everyone who runs toward him
makes it.'*

Psalm 18:30, MGE.

Make use of the route map.

---

*'The revelation of God is whole
and pulls our lives together.
The signposts of God are clear
and point out the right road.
The life-maps of God are right,
showing the way to joy.
The directions of God are plain
and easy on the eyes.'*

Psalm 19:7, 8, MGE.

God's word – the ultimate power pack!

'God's word is better than ...
a diamond set between emeralds.
You'll like it better than strawberries
in spring, ... There's more:
God's word warns us of danger
and directs us to hidden treasure.'

Psalm 19:10, 11, MGE.

In Death Valley God is your only strength.

---

*'Even when the way
goes through death valley,
I'm not afraid
when you walk at my side.
Your trusty shepherd's crook
makes me feel secure.'*

Psalm 23:4, MGE.

God is your Light and your Stronghold.

---

*'The Lord is my light and my salvation
– whom shall I fear?
The Lord is the stronghold of my life
– of whom shall I be afraid?'*

Psalm 27:1.

The prescription for salvation.

'In the gospel a righteousness
from God is revealed, a righteousness
that is by faith from first to last,
just as it is written:
"The righteous will live by faith." '

Romans 1:17.

The road to peace and joy.

'Therefore, since we have been
justified through faith, we have
peace with God through our Lord
Jesus Christ, through whom we
have gained access by faith into
this grace in which we now stand.'

Romans 5:1, 2.

God loves us *in* our sin, and *through* our sin, and goes on loving us, looking for a response.

'*What a wretched man I am! Who will rescue me from this body of death? Thanks be to God – through Jesus Christ our Lord!*'

Romans 7:24, 25.

For you to be in Christ,
Christ must first be in you. Is he?

_____

'Therefore, there is now no
condemnation for those who
are in Christ Jesus.'

Romans 8:1.

You can gain the victory.

'You have no obligation whatsoever to do what your sinful nature urges you to do.... But if through the power of the Holy Spirit you turn from it and its evil deeds, you will live. For all who are led by the Spirit of God are children of God.'

Romans 8:12-14, NLT.

The great day coming will eclipse
present sufferings.

---

*'What we suffer now is nothing
compared to the glory he will give
us later. . . . All creation anticipates
the day when it will join God's
children in glorious freedom from
death and decay.'*

Romans 8:18, 21, NLT.